MANNERS
AT THE TABLE

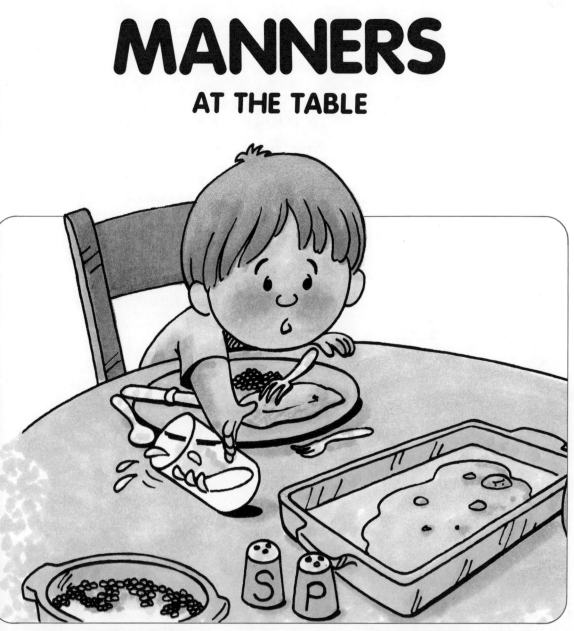

Written by
Alison Tharen

Illustrated by
Robert Elliott

MANNERS
SERIES

PUBLISHER	Joseph R. DeVarennes
PUBLICATION DIRECTOR	Kenneth H. Pearson
ADVISORS	Roger Aubin Robert Furlonger
EDITORIAL MANAGER	Jocelyn Smyth
EDITORS	Ann Martin Shelley McGuinness Robin Rivers Mayta Tannenbaum
PRODUCTION MANAGER	Ernest Homewood
PRODUCTION ASSISTANTS	Kathy Kishimoto Douglas Parker
PUBLICATION ADMINISTRATOR	Clare Adam
ILLUSTRATOR	Robert Elliott
COVER DESIGN	Sue Wilkinson

Canadian Cataloguing in Publication Data

Tharen, Alison, 1959–
  At the table

(Manners; v. 1)
ISBN 0-7172-2175-X

1. Table etiquette — Juvenile literature.
I. Title.   II. Series.

BJ2041.T43 1987   j395'.54   C86-095054-9

Manners are important because they show that you care about other people's feelings.

To be well-mannered at the table, you should know what to do if . . .
- you have to sneeze or cough
- you have more than one fork to choose from
- you don't like the food that is passed to you
- you need something you cannot easily reach
- you can't remember how to behave.

A list of "Do's and Don'ts" appears on the last page of this book.

It was almost dinner time. "Aunt Kathy has promised to take us to the circus if we behave and watch our manners," said Ashley.

"Oh boy!" cried Theodore. "I like the circus!"

"Me too," said Ashley. "So let's try extra hard to watch our manners at the table tonight."

"Dinner is ready," called Aunt Kathy. Ryan heard her, but he didn't get up. He was busy playing in the sandbox.

Ashley ran over to him. "Come on," she scolded. "Aunt Kathy called you to dinner. If we don't behave, she won't take us to the circus."

"OK, OK, OK," sighed Ryan. "Come on Bone," he yelled at the dog. "I'll race you into the house!"

Ryan and Bone ran toward the dining room. Ryan was laughing and shouting. Bone was barking and jumping.

Ashley put a finger to her lips. "Ssshhh!" she whispered. "Walk *quietly* into the dining room. But before you do," she reminded him, "go upstairs and tidy up."

Ryan washed his face and hands and straightened his clothes. Then he came quietly into the dining room.

Aunt Kathy came into the dining room carrying a large platter. "Go ahead and sit down," she smiled. "I just have one more dish to bring in."

Theodore began to fill his plate with everything in sight.

"No one should be served until everyone is sitting down," Ashley whispered. "Then help pass the dishes around the table. Remember to use the serving utensils to take the food out of the dishes."

Theodore waited for everyone to sit down. "I'll do what Aunt Kathy does," he thought. "That way I won't make mistakes."

Aunt Kathy picked up her napkin. She laid it across her lap. Theodore picked up his napkin and laid it across his lap. Ryan picked up his napkin and tucked it into his shirt. Ashley frowned at him and pointed at her lap.

Ryan took his napkin out of his shirt and put it on his lap. "I have two forks," he said. "Which one should I use?"

"Your dinner fork is the one *beside* your plate," said Aunt Kathy. "Your dessert fork is the one *above* your plate."

"Once you've used your knife and fork," Aunt Kathy reminded the children, "always set them down on your plate, not on the table."

She passed the peas to Ryan. "Yuck!" he cringed. "I hate peas!"

"If you don't like a dish," said Ashley, "just say 'no thanks' and pass the dish along." She leaned closer to her brother's ear. "You **do** like the circus," she whispered. "So remember, no manners, no circus."

Theodore took a bite of fish. Yeow! It was hot! He puffed his cheeks in and out like a fish. He flapped his hand in front of his mouth. He made such a fuss, he made Ashley frown.

"But it's too hot!" cried Theodore. "What was I supposed to do?"

"If the food is too hot and you've taken a bite, sip some milk," Ashley said. "Then wait until the food has cooled before you take another bite. Don't blow on your food. Just leave it until it has cooled by itself."

Ryan looked around the table for the salt. The salt was on the other side of the table. Ryan reached a-c-r-o-s-s the table and . . .

- C - R - A - S - H - !

He knocked over his milk glass. Ryan grabbed his napkin and began to wipe up the milk. "I know, I know, I know," he sighed. "Don't reach across the table. Ask for what you want to be passed to you. May I please have the salt?"

Theodore passed him the salt. "Now isn't that much easier than reaching across the table?" Aunt Kathy asked.

Ryan agreed. "And it's a lot less messy, too!"

"Tell me what you like about the circus," said Aunt Kathy.

Ashley and Theodore tried to tell her at the same time! Ashley tried to talk L-O-U-D-E-R than Theodore. Theodore tried to talk L-O-U-D-E-R than Ashley. Ryan kept interrupting both of them. Aunt Kathy tried to listen, but she couldn't tell who was saying what.

"CHILDREN!" she cried at last. Ashley and Ryan and Theodore stopped talking. "Only one person should talk at a time," said Aunt Kathy. "Everyone will get a chance to speak."

"OK," said Ashley, "we'll take turns. Theodore, you go first."

"I like the acrobats who swing way up in the air," he said. He swooped his hand into the pepper shaker as he spoke and knocked it over. The spilled pepper landed right in front of Ryan.

"Ah . . . Ah . . . Ahh . . . C-H-O-O!" Ryan gave a mighty sneeze.

"If you have to cough or sneeze," said Aunt Kathy, "turn your face away from the table and cover your mouth with your napkin. That way, you won't get germs all over the food!"

Ryan swallowed his last mouthful. "May I have dessert now?" he asked.

"When the rest of us are ready," said Aunt Kathy. "Meanwhile, just sit quietly, and wait for us to finish."

It wasn't easy for Ryan to sit quietly. Soon he began to fidget. He picked up his knife. Clink . . . clink . . . he hit it against his plate. TWING-ping . . . he hit it against his glass.

"Ryan!" said Ashley. "Aunt Kathy said to sit *quietly*. Stop fidgeting and don't play with the knives and forks."

Theodore didn't want to finish his peas. He pushed them around his plate with his knife. He pushed them into the middle and made a little pea hill.

"Don't play with your food," said Ryan.

"If you've finished eating," added Ashley, "then set your knife and fork down on your plate."

Theodore watched Aunt Kathy put her knife and fork down on her plate. She set them side by side on the bottom right hand corner, with the fork tines pointing up—so Theodore did the same.

Everyone got a slice of chocolate cake for dessert. Before Theodore had swallowed his last mouthful, he held up his plate and said, "More . . . please!"

Ashley sighed. "Don't talk with your mouth full. If you could see how awful it looks, you'd never do it again!"

Theodore swallowed his cake. "At least I remembered to say 'please'," he said.

"This cake is sure de-li-cious!" said Ryan. He took a big bite and smiled at Ashley. But Ashley wasn't smiling.

Ashley was frowning at Ryan's elbows. His elbows were on the table. Ryan slid them off the table. "Sorry," he said.

"You can rest your elbows on the table when you're not eating," said Aunt Kathy. "But no elbows on the table while you're eating."

Ryan felt a cold nose against his leg. Bone was hungry too, and Bone loved chocolate cake! He put his paws on Ryan's leg and started to whine. "You know I'm not allowed to feed you at the table," Ryan whispered. "Sit down and be a good boy."

Theodore noticed that there was quite a bit of chocolate icing on his fingers. He started to lick it off.

"Don't lick your fingers," wailed Ashley. "Use your napkin."

Theodore wiped his hands and placed his napkin on the left side of his plate just as Aunt Kathy was doing.

"May we please be excused?" asked the children.

"Yes you may," answered Aunt Kathy.

"I know we didn't do everything right," said Ryan, "but we tried hard to remember our manners. Will you still take us to the circus?"

Aunt Kathy smiled. "Yes, I'll take you to the circus."

"Oh boy!" cried the children.

"It's difficult to remember *every* table manner *all* of the time," Aunt Kathy added, "but if you remember the manners that we've learned here tonight, you'll always be well-behaved at the table."

Do's and Don'ts of Good Table Manners

- Come to dinner when you are called.
- Wash your hands and tidy up before coming to the table.
- Watch an adult if you are not sure what to do.
- Put your napkin across your lap.
- Wait until everyone is seated before serving yourself.
- Use the serving utensils to put food on your plate.
- Help pass dishes around, always passing to the right.
- Say "No, thank you," if you don't want a food.
- Rest your cutlery on your plate once you have used it.
- Turn your head away from the table and cover your mouth with your napkin if you have to sneeze, cough or burp.
- Ask someone to pass what you want if it is not nearby.
- If you would like some more, ask politely.
- When you have finished eating, lay your cutlery side by side across your plate.
- Use your napkin to wipe your face and hands.
- Put your napkin to the left of your plate when you have finished eating.
- Ask to be excused before you leave the table.
- Don't blow on your food if it is too hot.
- Don't mumble, shout or interrupt someone who is talking.
- Don't fidget at the table.
- Don't feed your pets at the table.
- Don't talk with your mouth full.
- Don't put your elbows on the table while you are eating.
- Don't play with your food or cutlery.